T5-AFY-410

A Gift For:

From:

Copyright © 2013 Hallmark Licensing, LLC

Published by Hallmark Gift Books,
a division of Hallmark Cards, Inc.,
Kansas City, MO 64141
Visit us on the Web at Hallmark.com.

Editorial Director: Carrie Bolin
Editors: Kara Goodier and Emily Osborn
Art Director: Jan Mastin
Designer: Mark Voss
Production Designer: Dan Horton

ISBN: 978-1-59530-907-5
BOK2149

Printed and bound in China

Aging
Gracefully

BY LINDA STATEN & JEANNIE HUND

They say that life is a journey and it's true. There's a lot to see and do, and the best way to catch the sights is to slow down and take a closer look. That's what aging gracefully is all about—liking who you are, appreciating what you've got, and knowing how to "have a nice day" every day! In your own unique way, of course. Join us as we celebrate the view from where we are now, and look forward to what's next.

When you were younger,
you never dreamed you'd just now
be hitting your stride.

Turns out, life isn't a sprint . . . it's an amble.

You're never too old to do something utterly immature.

(This is both good and bad.)

You're still a dreamer . . .

and you're definitely not the only one.

Even when our hands don't work
as well as they used to,
we'll always find a way to
make a peace sign.

Nobody gets to be our age
without a few dings.

It's no accident that confidence
and laugh lines arrive at
approximately the same time.

(They came cross-country in a Volkswagen van.)

By now, you know the words to about a million songs...

and that's not even counting the entire soundtrack of "Hair."
Hence, karaoke is your friend.

Once you hit a certain time in life,
"go with the flow" doesn't quite mean
what it used to.

Once groovy, always groovy.

(Hipsters got nothing on you, Babe.)

Contrary to your youthful fears,
the years have demonstrated that
no landslide can bring you down.

We showed the world
you could do anything
in blue jeans.

(And we're still showing them!)

Picket fences and picket signs;
they both made us who we are.

Peace, love, & rock 'n' roll
are still excellent ideas.

You're never too old
to have the time of your life.
(And you're part of the generation that's proving it.)

At any age, happy people
are beautiful people.

Do what makes you happy.

Time polishes away
rough edges and leaves
a charming patina.

And I'm not just talking about vintage furniture.

Your heart is more agile than it's ever been.
We just keep getting better at balance,
resilience, and loving life as it is.

As time goes by,
it's nice to finally realize
the one that got away
wasn't really the one you
wanted after all.

That dated old junk
stored in the basement
is now coveted, extremely cool
"Mid-Century Modern" décor.

Forgetfulness is not necessarily a bad thing . . .
especially when it comes to forgetting your diet,
your hang-ups, your ex, your to-do list, your age,
and your inhibitions.

Aging invites us to write our own rules
and define our own success.
In other words, do your own thing, man.

By now, you know a million secrets.
Some you keep, some you share,
and some still blow your mind.

Life is a road trip
with lots of good memories

and a few great detours you can't tell the kids about.

It's not the destination,
it's the journey.
Or, to put it more succinctly, keep on truckin'.

So often, the less flexible
we are on the outside,
the more flexible we are
on the inside.

Boomers don't age, they self-actualize.

(We really weren't kidding about feelin' those good vibrations.)

Life is a story with a surprise ending.

How much of a character you want to be is up to you.
If you want to live a long life, but you don't want to get old,
keep on having fun. As long as you're having fun,
you'll be full of life at every age.

No matter your age, always try to look forward in life.

Otherwise you'll just keep bumping into things.

You've been to hell and back,
and made pretty darn good time.

You're learning to be your own hero.

Which, as it turns out, is way more fun than being your own worst enemy.

Aging leads to that moment when you see
that all your so-called mistakes and missteps
led you to the exact place you needed to be all along.

We didn't like authority when we were young.
We don't like authority now that we're older.
You've got to admit, we're consistent.

Remember how we used to say,
"Do your own thing"? Well, now's the time!
Be unapologetically you. It's your right.
You've earned it.

At this point, taking the scenic route
(even if by mistake) is totally okay.

You still are, and will always be,

a wild thing.

When the clothes we wore
in our youth come back in style,
it isn't a sign that we're supposed
to wear them again. Really.

By 50, you've finally made friends with your body,
which is only fair, considering you've shared
some far-out times.

At a certain point,
it's clear who your real friends are.
They know you. They get you.
They find your questionable tendencies
endearing. You share a bond stronger
than anything life dishes up.
And you definitely know how to
make each other laugh.

We changed the world,
one great song at a time.

When you're older,
it's easier to forgive and forget.

Especially forget.

You are a child of the universe.

And in universe years, you're really young.

We can still look at life
through rose-colored glasses . . .
just as long as they're bifocals.

If we're lucky,

just as life gets harder on the knees,
it gets easier on the heart.

When you're young, you've got what it takes.
When you're older, you've still got what it takes.
You may not recall exactly where it is,
but you've still got it.

The longer your journey,
the more baggage you've got.

Which is actually good, because you need it
for all the cool stuff life gives you.

People are fascinating now . . . full of revelations, charms and quirks. The older we get, the more we enjoy the unique, mysterious characters of this world.

Getting older leaves more space for intrigue.
For cozying up to new ideas and unusual people.
Maybe this is just a fancy way of saying
the older we get, the less it's all about "me."
Sure does make the world a more interesting place.

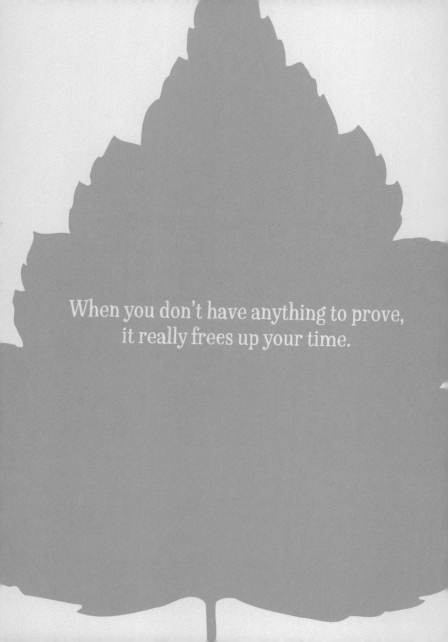

When you don't have anything to prove,
it really frees up your time.

Experience is the best teacher,
but it definitely gives too many tests.
But, I've got to admit, they've shown me my own strength.
As it turns out, I'm pretty much a badass.

Of all the things I've cultivated,
contentment is most rewarding.

At some point, you realize
that doing what you love
isn't a crime. In fact,
it's really good for you.

Certain things have stood the test of time . . .
peace signs, road trips, and the buddy system,
for starters.

These days, you are free to go placidly amid the noise and haste, and remember what peace there is in napping.

One day you wake up and realize
that you're more curious than judgmental . . .
more adventuresome than afraid.
And you think, wow, getting older
is a pretty good deal.

To keep life interesting,
try doing one thing every day
that embarrasses your kids.

You still totally rock
(so what if it's in a chair).

Life rolls along, and we roll with it.
The trick is rising to the challenge.
The reward is enjoying the ride.

Cookies made for grandkids
are way better than any other cookies.

Old age may come
knocking on our doors,

but if we turn up our classic rock,
maybe we won't hear it.

You dare to laugh in the face
of extended warranties.

There is a certain age when society begins to refer to us as "mature," which only proves once again that society doesn't have a clue.

It's nice to stop and finally smell the roses
we spent so much time planting in our youth.

Aging gracefully

is a close cousin to aging gratefully.

With age comes the wisdom to know
that some things in life can't be explained.
Like macramé.

We changed what it meant to be young.
Now we'll change what it means to be old.
Damn, we're good.

One of the best things in life
is having people you love
to grow wrinkly with.

And the beat goes on.

If you have enjoyed this book
or it has touched your life in some way,
we would love to hear from you.

Please send your comments to:
Hallmark Book Feedback
P.O. Box 419034
Mail Drop 100
Kansas City, MO 64141

Or e-mail us at:
booknotes@hallmark.com